ELECTRIC LOCOMOTIVES ON BRITAIN'S RAILWAYS

GEORGE WOODS

AMBERLEY

First published 2023

Amberley Publishing
The Hill, Stroud
Gloucestershire, GL5 4EP

www.amberley-books.com

Copyright © George Woods, 2023

The right of George Woods to be identified as
the Author of this work has been asserted in
accordance with the Copyrights, Designs and
Patents Act 1988.

ISBN 978 1 3981 0201 9 (print)
ISBN 978 1 3981 0202 6 (ebook)

British Library Cataloguing in Publication Data.
A catalogue record for this book is available from
the British Library.

Origination by Amberley Publishing.
Printed in the UK.

Introduction

The earliest major electrification network in the UK were the Southern Railway routes from the London terminals serving Sussex and Surrey, which were converted in the 1920s and 1930s utilising the third rail 660v DC system, with electric multiple units providing the services. Three 1470 hp Co-Co electric locos, 20001/2/3, were built between 1941 and 1948 to a Southern Railway design, becoming BR Class 70 for use on freight trains and the heavier boat trains to the Channel ports. These locos played a part in the development of future designs such as the Class 71. They were all taken out of service in late 1968 and early 1969.

In the late 1950s, the lines from London to the Kent coast were being electrified and required locos to work parcels and freight trains, plus the Night Ferry and Golden Arrow services, so twenty-four Class 71 2552 hp locos were built at Doncaster Works, which came into service in 1959. By the late 1960s, the traffic these locos were employed on was fast disappearing and ten were rebuilt as electro-diesels, becoming Class 74. Problems arose with the Paxman diesel engines, and as the boat trains to and from Southampton Docks that these locos hauled were becoming less frequent as we progressed into further into the jet age they became redundant in 1977. E5001 survives as part of the NRM collection.

There were still problems with live rails in yards and working the non-electrified routes, so in 1962 the Class 73 electro-diesels were introduced. These had 1600 hp in electric mode, with a 600 hp diesel engine for working off the juice, and proved very successful in service. A total of forty-nine of these versatile locos were built: the first six at Eastleigh, and the remainder by English Electric. These locos have been so useful that the majority of them are still in service some sixty years later, with only nine withdrawn from service.

The first electric locos built by British Railways after nationalisation were the fifty-eight 1500v DC EM1 Bo-Bo type (later Class 76) for freight traffic, and the seven EM2 Co-Co (later Class 77) for passenger trains on the Manchester to Sheffield and Wath lines. These locos were designed by Sir Nigel Gresley for the LNER, and one was built in 1941 and sent to the Dutch Railways in 1947 for trial running, seeing service there until 1952. The locos were equipped with electrical equipment by Metropolitan Vickers and built at Gorton Works, coming into service between 1952 and 1954. Freight traffic on the Woodhead Route was always very heavy, and various schemes to electrify the line date back to the days of the Great Central Railway but never reached fruition. The steep gradients on the climb to the Woodhead Tunnel from both directions made the line very difficult to work with steam locos, and the conditions on the footplates in the single bores of the Woodhead Tunnels were at best extremely unpleasant and at worst dangerous. Plans to electrify these lines were started in 1935 and work to install the gantries to support the overhead wires was almost complete in 1939, but the start of the Second World War caused work to be stopped until the war ended in 1945. Work resumed shortly after with the line opening in 1954, resulting in a tremendous improvement in the operation of the trains and conditions for the footplate crews.

The seven Class 77 locos worked the passenger trains until 1968 when they were all withdrawn from service. They were placed in store and eventually sold to the Dutch Railways in 1970, where they were used until withdrawn in 1985. Three have survived into preservation, 27003 is in the Dutch Railway Museum in Utrecht, and 27000/1 have been saved in the UK. The Class 76 continued giving reliable service hauling freight traffic, and after the withdrawal of the 77s also worked the passenger trains until these were withdrawn in early 1970. Traffic levels gradually decreased, and British Rail decided to concentrate freight traffic on the other two TransPennine routes, resulting in the closure of the line in 1981 and the withdrawal of the Class 76, which were sold for scrap with the exception of 26020, which is in the care of the NRM.

The 25 kV system of railway electrification was first employed by the Deutsche Reichsbahn experimentally in 1936, but further development was stopped in 1939. In 1950 it was adopted by the French railways as their standard system, being used to gradually rebuild and modernise their network after the destruction of the Second World War.

When British Railways announced its Modernisation Plan in 1955, they had decided to standardise all future electrification on the 25 kV system as it was seen as the most economic to install. The first lines to be modernised were the Great Eastern suburban system from Liverpool Street, completed in 1961, and the first main line to benefit was Euston to Birmingham, Manchester and Liverpool, completed in 1966.

The decision was taken to award orders to five British locomotive manufacturers to build a hundred 3300 hp locos of five different types suitable to work on the new system, which became classes 81–85. The locos were delivered between 1959 and 1963 and were put to work on the Manchester to Crewe line, which by then had been electrified. Much was learnt from these prototype locos, and the best parts from each design were used in the one hundred Class 86 locos built by English Electric and Doncaster works in 1965/6, becoming the workhorses of the new system. In the early 1970s it was decided to electrify through from Crewe to Glasgow, and this was completed in 1976. Thirty-six 5000 hp Class 87 locos were built by BREL at Crewe to work the extended services.

The East Coast Main Line was going to be the next electrification scheme after completion of the WCML, but political interference did not allow this to happen until a belated start was made in 1984. In 1976 the section between Kings Cross and Hitchin was completed as part of the Great Northern suburban electrification, but BR had to wait until 1991 when completion to Edinburgh and Leeds was achieved. As there were still parts of the East Coast services, such as those to Inverness, Aberdeen and Hull, not electrified, some services continued to be worked by diesel IC125 sets. The electric trains were powered by the thirty-one Class 91 Bo-Bo 6480 hp locos that were built by BREL at Crewe between 1988 and 1991, and are currently being replaced by Hitachi Azuma dual-powered multiple units.

The Class 89 was a one-off experimental 6000 hp Co-Co locos developed by Brush Traction and built at Crewe in 1986. At one time it was seen as possible power for the East Coast electrics but was heavier and less powerful than the Class 91. It was operated on the ECML in experimental service by both BR and GNER, but was taken out of use after a major failure in 1992. It has since been preserved and is now owned by a partnership between the AC Locomotive Group and Locomotive Services.

The forty-six 6760 hp Co-Co Class 92 locomotives were built by a consortium of ABB and Brush Traction between 1993 and 1996. These locos were intended to haul passenger and freight trains through the Channel Tunnel and were able to operate using power from 25kAC overhead wire and 750v DC third rail. Many of the intended services that the 92s were to haul either never materialised or were changed, which resulted in many of them being sold to other operators either in the UK or abroad. Approximately thirty remain in service in the UK, including six that are used on the Caledonian sleeper. Some are stored out of service, but about a dozen are used in Eastern Europe on freight services.

Class 88 is the first dual-powered (electric 5400 diesel engine 940 hp) electro-diesel 25k Bo-Bo to be built for a UK railway. DRS ordered ten from Stadler Rail and they were built in 2016/17. They are primarily freight locos, but can be used for passenger service as well. One of the first duties they have been used on is the heavy Daventry to Mossend Tesco container train, which climbs to the summits of both Shap and Beattock on its journey to destinations in Scotland.

Abbreviations

ABB	Asea Brown Boveri
ACLG	AC Locomotive Group
BRCW	Birmingham Railway Carriage & Wagon Works
DB	Deutscher Bahn
DRS	Direct Rail Services
ECML	East Coast Main Line
EE	English Electric
EWS	English Welsh & Scottish
GNER	Great Northern & Eastern Railway
LCGB	Locomotive Club of Great Britain
LNER	London North Eastern Railway
NRM	National Railway Museum York
RES	Rail Express Services
TMD	Traction Maintenance Depot
WCML	West Coast Main Line
VTEC	Virgin Trains East Coast
VTWC	Virgin Trains West Coast

92041 Vaughn Williams is seen at Carlisle station on 12 November 2007. Forty-six Class 92s were constructed to work trains through the Channel Tunnel and were named after famous European personalities associated with the arts.

20001 is seen in the fog at Wimbledon station while working the LCGB Sussex Venturer Railtour on 4 January 1969, which proved to be one of its last duties before withdrawal.

E6013 heads away from Woking with a parcels train in December 1966. Forty-nine of these electro-diesels were built in 1962, and have proved to be so useful that most of them are still at work in 2021.

New Forest ponies graze as E6037 descends Sway bank towards Brockenhurst and crosses the B3055 with a Bournemouth to Waterloo train on 14 June 1967.

73117 waits in Eastleigh station with a parcels train in September 1982.

73124 approaches Millbrook with a train for Weymouth in September 1982.

Above and below: Two views taken at London Victoria station showing, above, 73138 waiting to leave with a Gatwick Express service in June 1985, and, below, 73135 departing with the Venice Simplon Express Pullman train in August 1990.

73235 passes Clapham Junction station with a Gatwick Express which since privatisation has been operated by National Express. 3 October 2001.

The next three pictures were taken at the Eastleigh Works open day, which was held on 2 May 2009. The top picture shows 73006, which has since been rebuilt as 73967; in the middle image is 73109 Battle of Britain 50th Anniversary; and below is 73119 Borough of Eastleigh, both now in service with GB Railfreight.

73201 Broadlands, now with GB Railfreight, and two pictures taken at the Crewe open day held on 8 June 2019. The middle picture shows 73001, which is preserved at Crewe Diesel TMD, and below shows 73951 Malcolm Brindred, now in service with Network Rail.

E5001, in its original green livery, is owned by the NRM and displayed at Shildon, but seen here on display at the Doncaster Works open day held on 26 July 2003.

E5006 calls at Dover Priory station with a parcels train, 26 May 1971. Twenty-four of these locos were built in 1958, but due to lack of work ten were rebuilt in 1967 as electro-diesels, and the rest apart from E5001 were scrapped.

Above and below: Two pictures of electro-diesel 74007 at the Southampton Ocean Liner Terminal with a boat train for Waterloo, conveying passengers from the P&O cruise liner ORIANA, which is moored in the background. The loco will use its diesel engine in the docks until it reaches the main line, where it will change over to third rail electric for the journey to London.

26046 passes through Sheffield Victoria station on a murky November day in 1969 with a westbound freight for Mottram Yard.

The guard looks very lonely as he waits for departure time at Sheffield Victoria on 11 November 1969, but at least the few passengers will be warm if the amount of steam leaking from the train heating is anything to go by. 26055 Prometheus on the 11.45 departure to Manchester Piccadilly.

26055 Prometheus has just arrived in platform 1 at Manchester Piccadilly with a train from Sheffield Victoria on 11 November 1969. The steam heating boiler still seems to be working very well.

Above and below: Two more pictures of 26055 showing a cab view of the driver's controls, and a close-up of one of the nameplates, Prometheus, who in Greek mythology was a Titan and god of fire.

Another picture taken at Sheffield Victoria of the 11.45 service to Manchester Piccadilly, this time 26054 Pluto is in charge on 30 December 1969. The crew are probably discussing their futures as the passenger service finishes on 3 January 1970, and Sheffield Victoria station will be closed.

26021/26024 heads a coal train from the Yorkshire pits for industries in Lancashire through Dinting station on 11 November 1969.

26036 heads a westbound coal train towards Penistone station. At 750 feet above sea level, Penistone is the highest market town in England – and on 30 December 1969 one of the coldest.

Three Class 76 locos 76046/76014 and 76011 stand in Guide Bridge station waiting to back down into the sidings to pick up freight trains on 9 June 1977.

76013 passes through Darnall station on the outskirts of Sheffield with an empty merry-go-round coal train in September 1977. 76013 will work as far as Rotherwood sidings, where a change to diesel power will take place.

26020 has been saved by the NRM, and is seen here with 86214 Sans Pereil at the Rocket 150 celebrations held on 25 May 1980 to commemorate the Rainhill trials of 1829.

27002 Aurora has just arrived at Sheffield Victoria station on 1 September 1966 with a train from Manchester Piccadilly. After the Woodhead route passenger trains finished, the Class 77s were sold to Holland where they worked until withdrawn in 1985.

27000 Electra at the National Railway Museum York Rail 200 Railfest on 31 May 2004. 27000 normally resides at the Midland Railway Centre at Butterley.

81013 climbs past Greenholme on the ascent to Shap Summit with a Birmingham to Glasgow service in July 1989. This class were the first locos produced for the West Coast electrification, and twenty-five were built by BRCW entering service in 1959–64.

82001 was one of ten locos built by Beyer Peacock in 1960. Originally E3047, it is seen here at Glasgow Central station on 14 July 1976. It was scrapped in 1985.

82008 has been preserved by the AC Locomotive Group, and is seen on display at Crewe Works open day on 10 September 2005.

83007 waits to head south from Carlisle station with a parcels train on 21 November 1981. English Electric built fifteen of this type in 1960–62 and most were disposed of by 1993.

E3035 (83012) owned by the AC Locomotive Group at Doncaster Works open day on 26 July 2003.

84001 is seen here at the Doncaster Works open day, which was held on 26 July 2003. Ten Class 84 were built by North British in 1960, but because of problems they were out of service by 1980, and only 84001 survives as part of the national collection.

ADB968021 (84009) stands at York station in August 1990. It was rebuilt as a load bank tester, but was scrapped in 1995 by Gwent Demolition Margam.

85004 leaves Glasgow Central station with empty stock on 14 July 1976. Forty Class 85s were built at Doncaster in 1961–64 and were the most successful of the prototype 25 kV locos produced for the West Coast electrification working until 1994.

85023 arrives at Carlisle with a Motorail service for London in August 1982.

85015 climbs to Shap Summit, passing Greenholme with empty steel coil wagons and returning to Ravenscraig Steel Works in July 1989.

85101 (85006) has been preserved by the ACLG in Railfreight Distribution livery, which it never carried in service. Seen at the Crewe Works open day on 10 September 2005.

AL6 E3175 at Crewe station with a train for Euston in November 1971. Note the station signs – still in the Midland Region red colour scheme.

An AL6 (86) arrives at Crewe station with a northbound express in March 1972. These locos were the standard type built for the WCML electrification, and a hundred were built between 1965 and 1966 by EE at Vulcan Foundry and BR at Doncaster Works. Most have been scrapped but some are still in service with Freightliner hauling container trains.

86210 calls at Lancaster station with a Carlisle to Euston train in April 1976.

86246 passes Greenholme with a southbound tanker train in October 1978. Traffic on the M6 can be seen above the train in the left of the picture.

86031/86010 depart from Carlisle with a Freightliner service for Glasgow in April 1981.

86204 City of Carlisle calls at Birmingham International with a Wolverhampton to Euston train in April 1986.

86102 Robert A Riddles departs from Crewe with a Euston to Manchester service in August 1987.

Above and below: Two pictures taken at Crewe station in August 1987. Above, 86249 County of Merseyside passing through with an express for Euston. Below, 86245 Dudley Castle heads north with a Euston to Glasgow train.

Above and below: The next four pictures were taken at Crewe station in August 1987. Above, 86411 Airey Neave is arriving with a Liverpool to Euston service; below, 86432 departs with a Euston to Glasgow train.

Above and below: Above, 86217 Hayleys Comet stands in platform 5 with a train for Birmingham New Street and, below, 86103 Andre Chapelon heads another southbound service at the same platform.

86229 Sir John Betjeman heads north through the reverse curves at Low Gill with a Euston to Glasgow train in July 1989.

86102 Robert A Riddles speeds past the site of Scout Green signal box with a Birmingham to Glasgow train in July 1989.

86403 passes Greenholme with a Birmingham Glasgow service on a glorious July day in 1989.

86261 driver John Axon GC stands in platform 7 at Manchester Piccadilly station after arriving with a CrossCountry service on 12 October 1990.

Above and below: Two pictures taken at Carlisle station in June 1992. Above, 86425 receives some emergency repairs while working a southbound train, and, below, 86260 driver Wallace Oakes GC is at the rear of a southbound train. In the opposite platform, IC125 43069 is on a Plymouth to Glasgow CrossCountry service.

86434 JB Priestley OM climbs away from Oxenholme with a Birmingham to Glasgow service in June 1992.

86225 and a sister loco descend from Shap Summit past Greenholme with a Glasgow to Willesden Freightliner train in June 1992.

86259 Peter Pan waits to depart from Carlisle with a southbound express in June 1992. This loco has now been preserved.

86222 Clothes Show Live passes Low Gill with a Glasgow to Birmingham train on 16 July 1996.

86009/86600 pass Low Gill with a southbound Freightliner service on 3 May 1997.

86425 Saint Mungo is seen in York station with the Tyneside to Doncaster mail train in May 1997.

86417 has just arrived at Liverpool Street station with a service from Norwich in December 1998. Fifteen Class 86s were acquired by Anglia Trains, and worked until replaced by Class 90 locos in 2005.

Above and below: Two pictures taken a short distance apart in Cumbria show two Virgin Glasgow to Birmingham trains taken on 8 June 2000. 86244 The Royal British Legion speeds down Shap past Greenholme, and at Low Gill a similar train is headed by 86226 Charles Rennie Mackintosh.

86218 NHS 50 waits to depart from Liverpool Street station with a train for Norwich on 2 June 2004.

Four miles east of Liverpool Street lies the busy junction of Stratford, where 86217 City University passes with a Norwich to Liverpool Street train in September 2000.

Off its beaten track, 86223 Norwich Union passes Colton Junction on the outskirts of York with the return Anglian excursion from York to Ipswich on 6 April 2002.

86261 The Rail Charter Partnership is seen here in EWS livery at the Doncaster Works open day held on 26 July 2003.

86602 stands in platform 10 at York station on 13 November 2004 while employed on nighttime overhead wire de-icing duties.

86901Chief Engineer, formerly 86253, was used by Network Rail as a mobile load bank, seen at Carlisle station on 16 August 2006. This loco was eventually scrapped in June 2018 after being cannibalized for spare parts at Crewe.

Three pictures taken at the Crewe Works open day on 10 September 2005. 86604 in Freightliner livery; 86213 Lancashire Witch in InterCity colours alongside 87001 in BR Blue; and 86401 Northampton Town in Network SouthEast livery.

86622/86628 speed down the hill from Shap and are seen passing Greenholme on the approach to Tebay with a Freightliner train on 12 June 2006.

Just a few miles further south 86637 heads a short southbound container train through Docker on 25 September 2007. The sunlit Howgill Fells dominate the background.

Above and below: Two pictures of the Railtour which ran on 3 May 2008 hauled by 86259 Les Ross. Above, the outward leg passes Greenholme, and below the return trip is passing through Penrith station. 47773 (D1755) was on the rear.

Two more AC electric locos preserved by the ACLG are 86101 Sir William Stanier FRS (right), and 87002 Royal Sovereign, seen here at Carlisle station on 24 February 2012.

87030 waits to depart from Carlisle with a Euston to Glasgow train in March 1976. Thirty-six Class 87 locos were built at Crewe from 1973 until 1975 and worked WCML services until withdrawn in 2002. Some were sold to Bulgarian Railways, where they are still in service today.

87023 and 81005 are in the sidings at Wolverhampton station waiting to work their next trains on 5 June 1976.

87029 departs from Glasgow Central station with a train to Euston on 14 July 1976 as Class 303100 arrives with a local service.

87006 City of Glasgow is passing Greenholme heading for its namesake with a train from Euston in October 1978.

The driver of 87012 Royal Bank of Scotland washes his windscreen during the stop at Oxenholme station with a Carlisle to London train in July 1989.

87006 City of Glasgow climbs past Greenholme on a beautiful afternoon with a northbound express in July 1989.

87023 Velocity takes the through road at Crewe station with a Euston to Glasgow train on 15 October 1990. Unusually for a day service, the leading coach is a sleeping car.

87101 Stephenson backs onto a parcels train at Carlisle in June 1992. This loco was used to test Thyristor control equipment, and became the first Class 87 to be scrapped at Barrow Hill in January 2002.

The shadows are lengthening as 87007 City of Manchester assists 87030 Black Duncan through Greenholme with a late running Euston to Glasgow train after 87030 had failed further south on 16 July 1994.

87012 Cour de Lion about to depart from Warrington Bank Quay with a train for Euston on 4 April 2002.

87013 John O Gaunt approaches Winwick Junction with a Euston to Glasgow service on 31 May 2003.

Above and below: Two pictures of Virgin Trains services at Carlisle. Above, 87034 William Shakespeare is about to leave with a train for Glasgow on 10 June 2003. Below, 87024 Lord of the Isles departs with a train for London Euston on 25 June 2004.

Above and below: Two pictures of 87002, which was painted in Porterbrook colours. Above, it is at the Crewe open day held on 31 May 2003; below, it is at the next open day on 10 September 2005, named AC Locomotive Group.

87035 is lifted by the crane in the erecting shop at Crewe works during the open day held on 10 September 2005. At this time the remains of the works were owned by Bombardier, which had around a thousand employees.

87022 Cock of the North and 87028 Lord President wait to depart from Darlington station with the Darlington Community Festival Railtour on 23 September 2006. Both these locos were exported to Bulgaria for further work.

88004 Pandora passes Doncaster station with a morning freight train on 27 February 2019. The ten locos of Class 88 are the first dual-mode locos to be ordered by DRS and the first was delivered from Stadler Rail in 2016.

88005 Minerva on display at the Crewe Works open day on 8 June 2019.

89001 at the Doncaster Works open day on 26 July 2003 in GNER livery. 89001 is a one-off experimental 6000 hp Co-Co loco built by BR at Crewe in 1986 to a design by Brush Traction. It has run under a variety of different owners, and has been preserved by the ACLG.

90009 speeds up the gradient at Greenholme with an Anglo-Scottish service for Glasgow in July 1989.

In July 1989 90017 heads a Euston to Glasgow train through the colourful rosebay willowherb at Low Gill. The vans behind the loco are conveying cars using the Motorail service.

Almost brand new, 90014 passes Oxenholme station with the Crewe Works test train on a trial run in July 1989. Fifty of these 5000 hp locos were built for BR at Crewe works between 1987 and 1991.

90006 passes Low Gill with a southbound InterCity service in July 1989. The M6 motorway can be seen above the train, to the right of the picture.

Above and below: Two pictures of northbound expresses conveying Motorail vans at the head of the train. Above, 90010 275 Railway Squadron arrives at Crewe on 15 October 1990, and below 90001 BBC Midlands Today pulls into Carlisle in October 1991.

Above and below: Two views of Railfreight Distribution-liveried Class 90 locos in Cumbria. Above, 90035 Basford Hall descends Shap at Greenolme with a container train on 16 July 1996, and below a very lightly loaded 90131 Intercontainer saunters through Low Gill on 8 April 1997.

90026 Crewe International Maintenance Depot is seen at York after arriving with a special train, composed of the Rail Charter Services set of green Mk 1 coaches, from Kings Cross in August 2001.

90019 Penny Black is also at York but with the Tyneside to Doncaster mail train on 13 August 2002. This train along with others were operated for Royal Mail by Rail Express Systems until 2003, when Royal Mail stopped sending mail by rail.

90029 Frachtverbindungen (freightlinks) in German DB livery. This was one of three Class 90s painted in European railways' liveries. Seen here waiting to leave Crewe on 4 April 2002 with a southbound train.

90007 Keith Harper at the rear of a southbound express at Crewe on 4 April 2002.

A very shabby-looking 90040 is seen here at Edinburgh Waverley station in June 2001 after arriving with the overnight sleeper from London. It will lay over to work back to London on that night's train.

90004 City of Glasgow is seen in Virgin Trains livery passing Greenholme on its way to Glasgow on 8 June 2000.

Above and below: Two pictures taken at Doncaster station of the Tyneside to Doncaster Mail train, ran by RES. Above, 90040 The Railway Mission with 67010 Arrow just visible at the rear, both in EWS livery on 18 April 2002. Below, 90222 Freight Connection in Rail Distribution colours on 21 April 2002.

Above and below: Two pictures taken at Carlisle. Above is freshly overhauled EWS 90034 on a RES mail train heading for Glasgow on 6 August 2002, and below 90002 Mission Impossible is at the rear of a Glasgow Euston service on 10 June 2003.

Above and below: Two pictures taken at Liverpool Street station of Anglia Trains services for Norwich. Above, 90014 is in debranded Virgin colours on 24 April 2005, and below 90010 is in the new Anglia livery on 13 October 2005.

Above and below: The next four pictures show Freightliner Class 90s in three different liveries. Above, 90041 is in the first green livery entering Carlisle station with a southbound container train on 16 August 2006. Below, 90049, looking cool in the grey scheme, descends from Shap Summit through the reverse curves a Greenholme with another container service on 27 September 2006.

Above and below: Two pictures taken at Crewe on 8 June 2019. Above, 90044 is in Crewe station in grey. Below, wearing the second green scheme, is 90045, which is on display at the Crewe Works open day.

91004 The Red Arrows waits to leave York in November 1989, with a special charter train that started in Harrogate. This was one of the first Class 91-hauled trains to leave York.

One of the Red Arrows nameplates carried by 91004.

91020 is running blunt end leading as it waits to depart from York in October 1990 with a driver training trip.

91012 waits to leave York with a Kings Cross to Edinburgh train in September 1991.

Above and below: Two pictures take at Alnmouth in June 1992. Above, with a sea fret coming in off of the North Sea, 91003 speeds through with a northbound Anglo Scottish service. Below, another northbound train seen passing through Alnmouth station headed by 91016.

91004 The Red Arrows crosses the Royal Border Bridge at Berwick-upon-Tweed with an InterCity service for Edinburgh in June 1992.

91011 Terence Cuneo pushes hard at the rear of a southbound departure from Doncaster on 8 April 1997.

In its smart new GNER livery, 91025 waits at Leeds to start its return journey to Kings Cross in July 1997. The loco is running wrong way round; the blunt end should be coupled to the coaches.

91031 is approaching Colton Junction with a train for Edinburgh in June 1998. This loco was one of a few to carry the GNER insignia in white for short time.

91110 David Livingstone looks a bit the worse for wear in this picture taken at the Doncaster Works open day on 26 July 2003.

91118 Bradford Film Festival is on display at the Crewe Works open day held on 10 September 2005. Unfortunately it arrived so late for the show that it was not worth unloading it for proper display.

91004 is seen at Doncaster station on 28 April 1999, and has lost its The Red Arrows nameplates after repainting into GNER livery.

91118 Bradford Film Festival departs from Darlington with an afternoon train for Kings Cross on 17 September 2007.

Another Class 91 heads south for Kings Cross out of York in the golden light of late afternoon on 1 November 2006.

The appropriately named 91113 County of North Yorkshire stands in platform 9 at York station with a northbound train on 2 July 2004.

91125 Berwick Upon Tweed arrives at Glasgow Central with a train from London Kings Cross on 22 February 2008.

A Class 91 arrives at Leeds station with a train from Kings Cross on 18 September 2007. GNER doubled the service from one to two trains per hour in May 2007.

91118, which is still carrying the interim GNER/East Coast livery as late as 15 July 2013, is seen waiting to leave Leeds with a London train.

Above and below: In October 2006 GNER went bankrupt and the franchise eventually went to National Express, who operated the services under the name East Coast. The two pictures on this page show northbound trains at York station; above is 91114 on 27 May 2009, and below is 91101 on 17 September 2009. Both locos wear rebranded GNER livery, and at long last show the loco number on the front.

91121 Archbishop Thomas Cramner passes a Virgin Voyager as it pulls into Edinburgh Waverley station with a service from Kings Cross on 29 December 2006.

91117 is at the rear of a service to Kings Cross at Glasgow Central station on 25 February 2011. The service to Glasgow Central via the ECML finished later in 2011 when the Virgin Pendolino trains came into service on the WCML.

Above and below: Two pictures of trains in the new East Coast livery. Above, 91108 is on the 09.29 service to Kings Cross about to leave York on 6 June 2012, and below 91120 is at Leeds on the 08.45 service to Kings Cross on 15 July 2013.

On 7 July 2015, 91125 is seen at Doncaster wearing the East Coast livery with the Virgin logo overprinted. East Coast was operated by National Express from 2007 until 2009 when it had to give up the franchise. A new state-run East Coast company was formed to run trains until the franchise was awarded to Virgin Trains in 2015.

91132, in Virgin livery, speeds north through Doncaster on 25 February 2016. This loco was involved in both the Hatfield and Great Heck accidents when numbered 91023. Sadly this loco was the first to be scrapped after the introduction of the Azuma trains in 2019.

Above and below: Two pictures of 91111 For the Fallen, which in October 2014 was turned out in a special livery to commemorate the centenary of the end of the First World War. Three ceremonies were held at Newcastle, Leeds and Kings Cross to remember the many lives lost by the soldiers of regiments who came from towns and cities along the ECML.

Seen here at Doncaster on 27 February 2019 is 91110, which was named Battle of Britain Memorial Flight at the York Railway Festival on 2 June 2012 while the loco was in service with East Coast Railways. It also holds the speed record for the Class 91 – 162 mph – and has been chosen for preservation by the NRM when it is retired.

To commemorate thirty years in service, 91119 was repainted in InterCity Swallow livery by LNER and named Bounds Green in honour of the depot where the Class 91 has been maintained.

Two pictures of Class 91s in the Virgin Trains livery. Above, 91113 waits to leave Kings Cross on 17 August 2016 from platform 0, which was converted from the old cab road to provide much needed extra capacity. At the very left of the picture the remains of the tunnel entrance of the closed line that went down to Moorgate via the widened lines can be seen.

91125 at York station about to depart from platform 11 with a train for Kings Cross. 12 August 2016.

91131, now in what is basically the old VTEC livery but with LNER branding, leaves Doncaster with an afternoon train for Kings Cross on 27 February 2019. LNER is a government-run company set up to run trains on the ECML after VTEC had to give up the franchise in 2018.

91101 is seen here at Doncaster on 7 July 2015 in the first Flying Scotsman livery, which was applied while in service with East Coast Railways.

91101 in the second Flying Scotsman (Virgin) livery is preparing to leave Kings Cross with the 13.00 departure for Edinburgh on 17 August 2016.

91118 and East Midlands 43058 are being prepared for departure at Kings Cross station on 24 August 2017. The station had just been through a major rejuvenation that had taken five years to complete.

A view taken at Kings Cross on 2 June 2004 when GNER ruled the roost, and the station was largely as it had been for many years. Three Class 91s, and two HSTs are ready to start their journeys, but since this picture was taken a thorough renovation finished in 2012 has completely revitalised the station.

Twelve years later on 17 August 2016, East Coast are in charge and 91101 and 91102 wait to head north. The background has changed dramatically: the old buildings that date back to the building of the station in 1852 have been swept away, as have the gasometers, and the loco servicing yard has been replaced by soulless office blocks.

Another view taken on 17 August 2016 showing both of the train sheds, which were completely renovated, plus a new concourse and passenger facilities that cost £500 million and took five years to complete. 91101, 91102 and 91127 are ready for the off, but in the five years since this picture the new Azuma trains have almost completely taken over. *Plus ça change.*

A similar view but taken on 2 June 2004 from the other side looking towards York Way, which runs down the east side of the station. In 2020 further major work was completed to the approaches to the station with extensive track remodelling and the reopening of one of the tunnels.

Above and below: Two pictures taken at Greenholme on 8 June 2000. Above, 92035 Mendelssohn climbs past with empty HAA coal wagons bound for one of the Ayrshire collieries. Shortly afterwards, 92022 Charles Dickens in Railfreight Distribution livery speeds past towards Tebay with a southbound container train.

With 6760 hp on tap, 92017 Bart the Engine climbs effortlessly past Greenholme on 24 July 2010, with the thirty-two wagon Daventry to Grangemouth Tesco container train that at this time was operated by Stobart Rail.

Taken on 12 June 2006. by which time many 92s had been repainted in EWS colours, 92031 The Institute of Logistics and Transport heads for Shap summit with a sparsely occupied northbound container train.

92017 Bart the Engine is seen again with the Tesco container train, this time passing Little Strickland on the approach to Penrith on 31 July 2010.

Above and below: Two pictures taken at Carlisle Citadel station on 6 September 2006. Above, 92003 Beethoven waits on the middle road before running out to Carlisle yard to pick up a train. Below, 92024 JS Bach approaches the station with a short container train. The Class 92 was built to work freight and passenger trains through the Channel Tunnel, but passenger trains never started so they are to be found working the heavier freights on the WCML.

92001 Victor Hugo waits to take over an evening train at Carlisle station on 19 December 2007.

92015 in DB Schenker colours, heading the Tesco container train past the site of Scout Green signal box, is about halfway up the climb from Tebay to Shap Summit on 28 January 2012.

92002 HG Wells passes through Carlisle station on 27 June 2014 with a southbound container train. Note the murals on the station wall that depict scenes from the steam age at Carlisle.

92038 is seen at the Crewe Works open day held on 8 June 2019. The loco carries the Caledonian Sleeper livery. The loco worked the service between Euston and Glasgow.